Understanding Your *Depression*

RAY J. DODKINS

This Book is a work of fiction. Names, characters, places, and incidents
either are the product of the author's imagination or are used fictitiously.
Any resemblance to actual persons, living or dead, events, or locales is
entirely coincidental.

Ordering Information:

Prime Seven Media
518 Landmann St.
Tomah City, WI 54660

Printed in the United States of America

This book was penned by request from readers that read A. R. C. against depression and made claims of having saved their lives and rereading provoked personal thoughts, creating a better understanding of the Emotional triggers and there personal implications in each individual, But Comments about a much deeper explanation and more detail was needed to fill the personal understanding to a better level, So I have endeavored to fill this void with Understanding Your Depression. Your Personal Confidence and greater understanding of Self is my AIM Be kind to yourselves and Remember A Pain shared is Half the Pain and a Love shared is Twice the love.

Ray J. Dodkins

Men and women do not accept the word "depression" well, any more than we accept that our lives and emotions are out of our control.

The effect of depression is far greater on men than on women, because women are better equipped to adjust to major emotional upheavals.

Men, on the other hand, have great difficulty adjusting to new feelings brought on by major life triggers, which seem to be out of their control. In some cases, the feelings men have fought so hard to hide or suppress are now visible for all to see.

Displaying emotions threatens men's personal.

inner beliefs: who we think we are, and how our ideal man behaves and is respected.

Depression is a very debilitating mental illness, and the roller-coaster ride through emotional depression is neither expected nor accepted by men and women.

Men and women develop differently as children.

As boys develop, the figures they admire set their inner expectations for themselves as men, and Influence their Ideas of what a man does and does not do. Women, on the other hand, do not appear to have the same developmental pressures, and their aspirations focus mainly on body image and motherhood. Women's emotional makeup, including their capacity to deal with life's emotional upheavals appears to be far more flexible and adaptable than men's. On the surface, women are less judgmental of their inner selves and their reactions when faced with life's changes and emotional upheavals. Men, on the other hand, go into denial and make excuses for the dramatic changes in their outward actions.

For a man, any acceptance of a mental problem is not part of his perception that he is self-assured, in total control of life's happenings.

Depression undermines stability in life for both men and women. It pushes them outside of their comfort zones. When depressed, men become their own worst enemies. They become self-judgmental, and will not confront or talk about what can become a life-threatening mental disturbance. The reason for this denial in men, and sometimes women, is a lack of understanding of the circumstances in which they find themselves, and of the reasons why they are reacting and feeling differently than normal.

Men dismiss these changes, which confront their learned perceptions of who a man is, and how he reacts to and controls the situation. For women, acceptance appears to be far less disruptive, but is very threatening all the same.

First and foremost, the most important part of your emotional journey is to understand your personal head-space and think about the triggers that provoke the terrible thoughts of shame and self-judgment that come with the feeling of lost control. particularly in men. This desperate mental situation can be improved by understanding yourself, developing a greater confidence in who you are as an individual, and becoming aware that while depression is a personal problem, influenced by who you are as a person and how you react, the feelings are not isolated in you alone.

The reasons for these writings are to raise awareness and to engage in thought-provocation to look deeper inside men's and women's emotional development, and to examine the mental stimuli that influence their development from the start of life through puberty, in order to understand how these stimuli influence our very being and emotional existence.

Men react to thoughts that challenge their security in life. Have you ever wondered how you would react in a life-threatening situation? What would you do? Sometimes we pursue things that satisty our inner curiosity as to who we are as men and women. Rarely do we ask ourselves who we are and how we should react in different situations.

However, these unacknowledged challenges are always dormant in our development, although we do not understand how our inner thoughts develop and what fuels them.

Most cultures have an unspoken, natural consensus regarding the standärds for man- or womanhood Unconsciously men and Women absorb many ideas and emotions, and admire deeds that embody their ideals of manhood and womanhood. This process sets their inner standards of who they believe they are, and how they react to circumstances or events.

Emotional education starts at a very early age of development: Boys appear to be more adventurous in puberty than girls, and sometimes push the personal envelope in safety in order to test their own limits of endurance and survival against threatening situations. This process also sometimes involves sexuality, Within this developmental stage. boys are generally more adventurous sexually, and are very susceptible to male predators exploiting this sexual adventurousness. People are sometimes bewildered by the victim's unexplained failure to report molestation. One explanation for this phenomenon is that if the boy is made to feel involvement and pleasure in the act, he will in most cases say nothing He feels guilty and embarrassed by the act, and will later understand that it was wrong. Most molestation of girls is damaging and hurtful. Since in most cases girls are molested by someone they trust, their pain is often diminished and they are made to feel as though they were engaged in the abuse.

Any excitement felt, no matter how small, can trigger feelings of guilt and fear. People who engage in abuse are aware of how to take advantage of feelings, and sometimes attempt to normalize the abuse. Only by understanding the depths of inner turmoil from which we all suffer as we develop and grow will we be able understand such actions and hopefully prevent them from occurring or repeating in the future. These actions will build and create an emotional disturbance, leading to depression, self. judgment, and a deeper mental disturbance.

Understanding this experience will give a person a greater understanding of his or her true inner self.

Emotion, once experienced, is stored deep inside us. We carry emotional disturbance throughout our lives. Most events are totally out of our control, and some emotions have a lasting effect on us in many ways. These sometimes unfortunate experiences surface later in life. When compounded by emotional triggers, the onset of anxiety and depression is very strong, mainly because these events are old and cannot be changed or controlled!

The unacknowledged understanding of who we are and who we wish to be is different for everybody.

Our experiences influence our development and set our personal standards as men and women. Our inner, unaddressed thoughts are not generally recognized or understood, but their influence is within each and every one of us all the time. Inner thinking fuels our self-doubts and self-criticism of our reactions to emotional and Physical disturbances.

Events in our lives cause our inner feelings of lost control. This journey and these feelings threaten us personally, because we have not met our own demands and standards for ourselves. It is important and necessary to achieve a far better understanding of ourselves and how we live our lives. Thinking deeply into our own development may give us a better understanding and answers, thus enabling a progressive movement forward, away from emotional turmoll. This helps us understand others and ourselves, and develops stronger self-confidence In each individual.

You must remember that in life there will always be somebody to envy and admire because he or she appears to be more in control, more confident or more capable. Such thoughts are very self-judgmental. Remember that you do not know another person's limits in life, nor how they judge themselves and their capabilities. There is no "normal" or standard as billions of humans are equally and uniquely different

Explanations for what causes this depth of emotional turmoil are as numerous as there are people in the world. Put simply, we are all affected emotionally in many ways and to varying degrees.

Some small occurrences have major emotional effects, and major events are sometimes just dismissed, but all experiences add to what I think is an emotional "cup" deep inside ourselves.

Throughout life, we fill and empty this cup of feelings by relaxation and rest as well as by focusing on hobbies, sports, and work interests.

However, the truth appears to be that once the cup is overfilled with emotion, the effect becomes anxiety and depression, which threatens our comfort zone.

The comfort zone may not be ideal, but it is stable.

We adjust our lives to suit the demands that life places on us within this feeling of comfort. The emotional ride after living with and overcoming depression is at best very challenging mentally, and is the most unhinging experience in many people's lives.

Emotional triggers are slow and consistent, and add to the filling of our cup. Because we as individuals are affected differently, threats or triggers are different for everyone. The threat to each person's Inner ideal self is different.

Therefore, In some cases, a small incident can be threatening to some individuals and minor to others. Because the life experiences we have gained and observed in our development are all different, so are our expectations of who we are as individuals. Emotion, once experienced, is stored deep inside us, and we carry this disturbance through our lives, Most events are totally out of our control, and some emotions have a lasting effect on us in many ways.

This places us in a space that we do not understand or can control, and our comfort zone is turned upside down. This is not because of the situations themselves, but rather because of our reactions to the triggers, the excuses we make for our reactions, and our expectations for ourselves regarding how we react to these circumstances.

The second-most important point is recognition - the recognition that we are affected by outside influences, and that we as individuals have no control over when and how these events affect us, not to mention the behavioral changes they cause, which we struggle to hide and make excuses for.

Life after depression is different for each man, and even more so for women.

The feeling of protecting your inner self has not changed, but most men still try to hide the emotions that are now so close to the surface. Emotional expression is more accepted in a woman. After the emotional cup inside oneself has been filled and overflows, now, with help, it has been emptied. It will easily be filled again with further experiences. Without understanding and control, this will again lead to a major emotional upheaval and disturbance. For women it is different, but when men experience something emotionally affecting, they find themselves trying to suppress the urge to express emotion. They start explaining the tears as sore eyes, due to inner beliefs that real men don't cry, but their natural instincts and feelings have not changed. These explanations work sometimes, so that you do not feel threatened as a man. However, close friends and loved ones may notice the denials and excuses. In women, this dental is generally not as acute, and is more likely to be accepted.

How often have you thought about some seemingly successful person who has committed suicide? Sometimes we are bewildered by that person's apparent sellishness. Such events are brought about primarily by the triggers of life, and people seem to have lost control. They feel that the problem is out of control and they cannot fix it, so they doubt themselves. The threat is now their own inner assessment of who they are as people, After trying to work harder and longer, they have found that the problem will not go away. This sets the stage for becoming depressed. Sometimes, to accept the reasons for actions is to develop a better understanding of what appear to be unexplained actions and judgments. These actions in life will bulld and create an emotional disturbance that will establish a foundation for depression, as well as contribute to more self-judgment and a deeper mental disturbance. Understanding this experience will give you a greater understanding of your true inner self. Once taken to that extreme level of emotional disturbance, the feelings and reactions that we have fought so long to either hide or control are now and forever closer to the surface than ever before. This road of emotlonal turtoll has been travelled by both men and women, to varying degrees of effect.

A fact not readily recognized is that women are far better equipped to deal with emotional upheavals in life. Men, on the other hand, receive life-long perceptions as very small boys and all the way through puberty of who they are as men, how they can. earn respect and trust, and how they can be admired by others,

Slowly induced emotional and physical impressions during childhood have life-long effects on how we react and what we do in our journey to manhood or womanhood. Any drastic, sudden changes to our stability in life and our comfort zone are threatening, and can give rise to a perceived loss of control over our lives. The emotional triggers provoked by any number of illnesses or disturbances In life can trigger reactions in anybody. For example, we might be in denial of the effects of an accident, a medical diagnosis, or a separation from a partner, whether temporary or permanent. Any event can trigger emotional disturbance and depression.

Influences on development are as strong for young giris as they are for young boys, but it would appear that the personal burdens young women place on themselves are far less demanding Everlasting female influences affect all men, and because we all have female hormones, sometimes female influences arise in life. Men feel challenged or threatened because they do not understand the female feelings that are strong in some circumstances. They dare not show these feelings or fall prey to them, because it threatens them as men.

Have you ever wondered why men seek challenges in their occupations and hobbies that seem dangerous and life-threatening? Such tasks challenge our unspoken fears of how we will react when scared, or if our life stability is threatened. Men set these challenges for themselves. In most cases, when asked, people will say they are motivated by the adrenaline rush or high caused by the challenge and accomplishment. However, in truth, these men and women are trying to satisfy their own deep, unspoken doubts as to who they are and how they overcome their fears and perform when put to the test. These endeavors will persist on many levels as we try and obtain the self-acceptance and confidence we need as individuals. Daily life struggles will persist until we become emotionally satisfied with where we are and who we have become.

Men have a need to be recognized as exceptional in some endeavor. Accomplishment further fulfills the Inner need for self-confidence and the simple, special feeling about oneself. Women feel the same way, but their inner expectations are different than those of men. Sometimes, women have life-threatening and unexplainable body image issues and are sometimes consumed with self-criticism and judgment. This causes eating disorders and threatens their lives One of the most difficult circumstances for women is the loss of one or both breasts, not to mention hysterectomy. These things undermine their inner expectations of being a woman, and affect how they think they are seen and judged.

When we are given help and understanding, we need to think through and address unacknowledged Ideas, and understand our personal uniqueness as humans. We slowly understand how we developed and formed these inner, unspoken ideas of who we are, how we should look, and how we should react to different experiences in life. This will in some cases relleve the inner turmoll and self-judgment.

The average man or woman goes through life wanting the security of a home and family. Some men are brought up with a work ethic that requires them to supply all the funds necessary to maintain the family home, as well as try to excel in many other areas. This ethic adds to an emotional burden at some level. Any disturbance to this endeavor adds to daily stress and emotional upheaval.

Sadly, some men and women never achieve self-acceptance and understand their own worth.

When they meet a person who seems to have all the things that they aspire to have and to be, and who appears confident, it is difficult not to admire who. that person seems to be outwardly. They express admiration and aspire to obtain and project that confidence. Women have different expectations and motivational desires than those of men, but they still try to compare themselves to others.

Remember that the people you admire are subject to the same emotional fears as you are, and may not have had the grounding male and female examples that have influenced your life and emotional development. They could be hiding some deficiencies in their minds, outwardly projecting what you see and admire to cover their inner judgmental feelings.

All children are greatly influenced by the adults who surround them, including family members. In most circumstances, we do not consciously absorb the details of our lives' development, but these details affect each and every one of us.

They are the emotional building blocks for life and personal presence.

Related to this process is one possible explanation for why we judge ourselves so harshly and refuse to talk and seek help. We make excuses for the effects of depression and anxiety on our lives and actions.

We make excuses to explain the changes in our behavior that we make to offset the effects of depression and anxiety. We become unyielding in our acceptance of the effects of depression and the threat it poses to our lives security and our well-being. Dealing with the threat to our inner, personal selves and personal beliefs requires counseling and help with moving on with our lives and returning to our comfort zone. Sadly, counseling does not supply answers to unspoken questions, but simply supplies tools to readjust your life.

The experience of depression is caused by many factors and the emotional events that are ever so slowly added to our little cup. The more emotion we feel, and the sadder the events, the more pressure builds up, which seems out of our control. This creates a spiral effect, and we slip slowly into emotional changes that thrust us into deeper areas that put huge emotional burdens on ourselves. We tend to treat these burdens as though they are physical, and can be adjusted or controlled. If this situation remains unchecked, it threatens our positive self-image. We become anxious, then depressed. We do not seem to match the level of demand on our physical and emotional selves, thus, the feeling that we lack control.

One of the hardest things to get our heads around is that at the other end of this demanding journey, when we confront the changes and accept the good and bad situations, we realize that our judgment of ourselves is invalid and slowly regain control of our lives. Now, the new journey begins, as we take control of our lives and slow the pace of our daily activities. We make mental adjustments to slow down our endeavors, to make up for what we believe has or has not taken place, or been affected by our now-recognized illness. Without help, some men and women will not survive the sickness of depression.

So the last and final important point is that we can now regain control of our lives and emotions, giving us a means of survival in the direst mental place we can find ourselves in life.

Surprisingly, we think we are alone and cannot talk to anybody about our uncontrolled feelings. We feel that to admit these deep, unspoken personal Ideas is embarrassing, so we should not speak about them. But when we realize that this judgment is incorrect, we understand that it affects not only us, but impacts everyone at some stage in varying degrees. People both close and distant all suffer from personal judgments. Rather than criticize your dilemma, they will often prove supportive of you as a fellow human being

Strong caring, and understanding people can be more helpful and supportive than we could possibly have imagined.

Other people are willing to help and support. This should teach us all that others do not look down on us because we have human frailties and misunderstandings. respect we have fought so hard to earn and maintain is threatened from within, rather than by outside sources.

In fact, the way you handle this journey could aspire other men and women to admire your reactions and outward presence. The way you handle your triggers and experiences can pass on inner strength. Thus, in turmoil, we have unknowingly set the bar a little higher and promoted a standard for personal respect in other men and women as well as in ourselves. It is not difficult for close friends and people you love and admire to observe the emotions and events that have affected you and how you have handled the journey.

Challenging events are part of a growing and learning phase in your life's journey. However, our feelings can become overwhelming and easily get out of control, even when we have a greater understanding of them. Sometimes further support is needed.

Our desire to be a specific type of man or woman makes us at times our own worst enemy. We critique who we are as men and women as individuals. We must accept the fact that we have an inner desire to be a different person than who we perceive we are.

Sometimes this is the motivation and drive that pushes us to achieve levels of acceptance and excellence in our chosen fields, such as politics, medicine, commerce, or trades.

Depression is an illness and does not affect everybody in the same way. It seems to depend on how many emotional changes we are subject to in life, and how intense they are in the scheme of things.

These emotional triggers disturb your comfort zone.

For those who are lucky to be in the small minority of confident people, these triggers do not appear to have as great an effect. Such people deal with the turmoil differently.

The loss of someone emotionally close to us, whether by absence or death, is and always will be life-changing in its effect on a person, especially coupled with the daily stress we experience, and the commitments we place on ourselves as a society, It is very good to try and understand what changes us and influences our judgment and stress levels.

Gaining this understanding is the best preventative tool you can have in your mind as you attain awareness of the emotional influences that affect your space and mind

Recognizing all of these changes, no matter how large or small, will stop their overwhelming effects on our mental state and their catastrophic effect on ourselves and our families, not to mention on our close friendships. Being aware of the journey of depression and its pitfalls should empower us to avoid repeating the episode and to move forward to happy, fulfiling lives.

Living the Journey and suffering the draining emotional turmoil does make us stronger, even though repairing the damage is slow and gradual. Although it is challenging at times, many have lived and survived the emotional road of depression.

Now, in this stage of the emotional journey, we can take control of our lives and help both ourselves and others. The rewards of sharing the developed understanding of this illness are extremely satisfying, both for your own emotional reassurance and for the effective assistance you can pass on to somebody else. The gratitude generally expressed by others is enormously rewarding to your rebuilt self-esteem.

You may derive confidence from the reassurance of sharing your emotions and your journey. Having somebody relate to how you feel is in itself very rewarding

The Important move away from expecting control over our comfort zone and circumstances in our lives, and away from the inner judgment of your perceived shortcomings, will bring a greater self-confidence in the secret you. With luck, the ogre of depression will have a much lesser influence, both now and in the future.

In summary, getting help from actively engaged professionals is excellent. However, for unknown reasons, professionals give you the tools to get on with life and move ahead without explaining the reasons behind the life experiences ingrained into a person's mind, and the childhood development that leads to denial. Obtaining answers and understanding is not easy, but if these writings can trigger some inner thought and understanding, then it's possible to reach a broader understanding that will lessen the emotional burdens we place on ourselves. Because each person has many different experiences, and each individual is affected differently by different circumstances, a lack of self-confidence and control can also result in the anxious or depressed person physically lashing out at the person closest to him or her. There is no single answer, and at best, we gain strength in sharing our thoughts and fears with caring people, thus enabling a progressive movement forward and away from emotional turmoil to assist in understanding others and ourselves, and developing stronger self-confidence.

I believe that reaching a better understanding of who we are and what we expect from ourselves, as well as achieving self-confidence, enables us to obtain what would normally seem impossible. This is a way forward to dealing with the unexplainable events in all of our lives, so that our dally learning process is fulfilling and rewarding. Remember always that a love shared is twice the love, and a pain shared is half the pain.

I hope this book makes you stronger and always gives you hope.

Ray J. Dodkins

Review Requested:
If you loved this book, would you please provide a reviewe at Amazon com?

Living after Depression. For Men & Women   By
Ray J Dodkins.

The emotional ride after living with and
overcoming depression is at best very confronting
mentally and emotionally, and is the most
unhinging experience in many ways to all who
experience it in life and survive. The triggers are
slow and consistent and add to the filling of our
emotional cup, these experiences are sometimes
minor and there are others that are major emotional
upheavals in our life. Because we as individuals
are effected differently and the emotion once
experienced is stored deep inside us either in part
or whole, and we carry this disturbance through
our life in what I like to call our little emotional Cup
and this cup fills and empties with rest and hobby
activities and when the triggers of life become out
of control and the cup overfills we are now out of
control. Most of these events are totally out of our
control and dissipate with time and relaxation and
we are unaware that these emotions have made

a lasting effect on us in many ways. Because of our deep unspoken development as humans and onto being the developed person we desire to be. These experiences and resulting perceptions varies from person to person and are greatly influenced by our development from childhood, and in most cases depending on what we have experienced the inner threat to our personal ideas as to whom we are as individuals. Life is at best full of things that disturb the most stable of humans; all the small occasioning events of daily life add to the stress levels. Some totally unknown and many others very much in your face, these are the circumstances that collectively set you into Anxiety and Depression in the first place.

The deeper meanings are the standards we as people set for ourselves and when these events confront us we rebel emotionally with defensive approaches and denial, the reason is simple, these sets of circumstances are confronting our personal images' of who we are and who we think we are and they undermine our control and eat away at our own self doubts. Not because of the situations but major step to excepting our life, our reactions, denials and the expectations we react to the circumstances presented, understanding this after Depression is different because our perception of how the real human person deep inside of us would or should react too. Excepting that once taken to that extreme level of emotional disturbance, that the feelings and reactions we have fought so long to either hide or control are now and forever more closer to the surface than ever before. Life after Depression is different for each person. The feelings of protecting your personal inner self have not changed but most people still try to hide the emotions that are now so close to the surface. After the emotional cup inside one's self has been filled and overflows, and now through help & rest has been emptied. Will easily be filled again with further experiences and without understanding and control will become a major upheaval and disturbance again. Now experiencing something at any time that is emotionally moving, you find yourself trying to suppress the out of control emotion, you start explaining the tears as sore eyes, this is your inner beliefs of the person you actually are. One of the things in life is that real men don't cry and your natural instinct and feeling have not changed no matter what.   But on the other scale Women can and do express emotional events a lot more freely and for some reason appear to be far better emotionally under control than men but the inner effect is as strong as with every human. The understanding and acceptance that once subject to the depths of depression and discovering some understanding of the denial and excuses made about circumstances and actions that close friends and loved ones have noticed, and you have experienced is now giving a greater understanding of your true self worth. This road of emotional turmoil has been travelled by both men and women at all levels of effect in their lives and a fact not readily recognized is that women are far better equipped to deal with these emotional upheavals in life. Men on the other hand obtain lifelong perceptions as very small boys on and upward through Puberty about whom they are as Men in life, and how they can earn respect and trust as a very individual persons being a special man or women, to be admired by other Men and women, it is this slow induced emotional and physical impression on a developing person that have long life lasting effects on how we react and what we do in our journey to maturity. Not forgetting the everlasting Female influences that effect all men and because we all men have female hormones as well, sometimes the female influences that arise in life depending on how they are presented, also can make us feel threatened as men and because in some circumstances our female feelings are strong and we dare not show or fall prey to this because it threatens our perceived understanding of whom we are as respected individual human beings MEN or WOMEN. The average Man & Women goes through life, and most want the security of a home and family some people are brought up with a work ethic that requires them to supply all the funds to maintain the home for the family. As well as try to excel in many areas in life, this ethic also adds to an emotional burden at some level. Any disturbance of this endeavor adds to the daily stress happenings and emotional build up inside. Have you ever wondered why some people seek challenges that sometimes seem dangerous and life threatening? These tasks are to challenge our unspoken fears of how we will react when our life is put under threat , most become disjointed and scared, and then our life stability is threatened, these reactions are self set and in most cases when asked most will say " it's the adrenal rush or high caused by the challenge and accomplishment " in most cases that is a true belief and an acceptable explanation, but in truth the deep unspoken and never said feelings are that these people are trying to satisfy their own doubts of how in control they are and how they overcome their fears and perform when put to the test. These in devours will persist on many levels to try and obtain life stability; the struggles will persist till we become emotionally satisfied with where they are and who they have become. To be recognized as exceptional in some endeavor, this accomplishment further seals the inner needs for self confidence and the simple feeling special about one`s self. Sadly some people never archive this self acceptance of their own worth and when they observe and meet other people that seemly have all the things that they aspire to have and be, for an individual to show this admired level of confidence whether it is in or out of the emotional high or lows, it is difficult not admire the person that appears to express and show outwardly the confidence and aspiration to promote the confidence we need as humans, to deal with these daily life emotional triggers.

Remember they too are subject to similar emotional fears as you and may not have had the grounding or general examples that have influenced your life and emotional development. They could be then hiding some self awareness of deficiencies in their mind and outwardly project what you see and admire. All children are greatly influenced by the surrounding adult people both involved in our upbringing and by association with family when we are growing up. And in most circumstances we do not consciously absorb the details of life's development but all these circumstances effect each and every one of us with emotional building blocks for life and personal presence. When we are growing up. And in most circumstances we do not consciously absorb the details of life's development but all these circumstances effect each and every one of us with emotional building blocks for life and personal presence.

The Depression experience is caused by many factors in life and the emotional events ever so slowly added to our little cup, the more emotion we become involved in and the sadder the events and more seemly out of control pressures we are subject to. This creates a spiral effect and we slip slowly into emotional changes that thrust us into deeper areas that put huge emotional burdens on us, if this situation remains unchecked it threatens who we perceive ourselves as an admired person and we become depressed. Part of this problem some people find that they need to work harder to solve the out of control situation we find ourselves in, (i.e.) we do not seem to match the level of demand on our physical and emotional selves thus the lost control feelings.

So one of the hardest things to get our heads around is that at the other end of this demanding journey we confront the changes and except the good and bad situations and now slowly we regain control of our life. Now the new journey begins. We then try to pace of our daily activities, the mental adjustment to slow down our endeavors to make up for what we believe has or has not taken place or been affected by our now recognized illness. Yes believe this is a sickness that unaided in some way, some people will not survive. Surprise is that when we thought we were alone and could not talk to anybody about these uncontrolled feelings. There are people, both close and distant more supportive of us as fellow human beings, stronger caring and understanding people more helpful and supportive than we could have possibly imagined. Although their understanding may not be compete they are all willing to help and support, this should teach us all that we are not looked down on as a person because we have human frailties and the respect we have fought so hard to earn and maintain is not threatened. In fact the way we handle this journey depending on the triggers could inspire other people to admire your reactions and outward presence.

This is in part how you have handled these experiences, thus in turmoil we have unknowingly set the bar a little higher and promoted a standard for understanding in other people and ourselves, it is not difficult for closes friends and people you love and admire to have observed the emotions and events that have affected you and how you have handled the journey. These events in somebody's life are a growing and learning phase of our life's journey. Although these feelings can become overbearing and easily out of control, even with a greater understanding, Sometimes further support is needed. Sometimes we will have noticed that our previously suppressed emotions are now very close to the surface and are more difficult to hide and control so in some way now we are in a mental area that we fought generally to hide and keep deeply secret. This level of confidence to control these feelings is very difficult to archive for some, because no matter how good we are at some things we all have self doubts about our ability and presence. Travelling down the emotional trail of depression leaves a lasting mark on most people both men and women alike that have suffered and survived, your feelings are at best ripped raw and now linger so close to emotional surface that unexpected happenings both physical and emotional will bring past experiences to the surface, because of the journey and the understanding now learned the adjustments to control and manage these seminally impossible situations are now much easier to embrace with control and understanding and the effect on our emotions far less than before. One thing to remember is the learning experience and the personal awareness is not generally understood and in some cases people do not comprehend the depth of inner understanding.

Reflecting on this desire to be a specific type of person we are at times our own worst enemy, critiquing who we are as a person and our perceived worth, but having stated this we must also accept the fact that this inner desire to be a different person than who we perceive we are!   Sometimes is the motivation and drive to become an influence and respected in circumstance and endeavors we are confronted with in life.(i.e.) Politics, Medicine, Commerce, Trades. Depression is an illness and does not affect everybody the same way it would appear it seems to depend on how many Emotional changes we are subject to in life and how intense they are in the scheme of things.

It would appear that the major loss of somebody emotionally close either by absence or loss of life is and always will be life changing in its effect on a person, couple this with the daily created stress and commitment we have placed on ourselves as a society, it is very good to look outside the square and understand what changes us and influences' our judgment and stress levels, gaining this understanding is the best preventative tool you can have in your mind. This could create an Awareness of the emotional changes and influences' on our own space and mind.

Recognizing all of these changes no matter how large or small will stop the overbearing results on our mental state and the catastrophic effect on ourselves and family not to mention close friendships, being aware of the journey of depression and the pitfalls to oneself should empower us not to repeat the episode and move forward to a happy for filling life and having lived the journey and suffered the draining emotional turmoil , does make us stronger even though repairing the damage is slow and progressive but many have lived and survived the road, although a little disturbing at times.

Now in this stage of the emotional journey we can take Control of our life and both help ourselves and others because the rewards of sharing the developed understanding of this illness is extremely satisfying both for your own emotional reassurance and the effective assistance passed on to somebody else, the gratitude generally expressed is enormously rewarding in re won self esteem and well derived confidence also the reassurance of sharing the emotion and journey having somebody relate to how you and they feel is in its self very rewarding. In summary all the help from actively engaged professionals is excellent but for some unknown reasons they give you tools to get on with life and move ahead, but the reasons and understanding the of life`s expectations ingrained into a person's mind and development that causes the denial of the things experienced are not explained. Because each person has as many different experiences as there are people in the world.

The reason for this writing is to engage in thought provocation to look deeper inside our emotional development and mental stimulus during development from the start of life and on through puberty, and how this influences everyone's very being and emotional existence. And generally we are own worst emotional enemy, have you ever wondered how you would react in a life threatening situation? Sometimes the pursuits we engage in are to do just that, just to satisfy the inner curiosity of whom or what we perceive we are. Rarely do we think of who we believe we are or who we perceive we are and how we should react in different situations, not at all understanding how these inner thoughts developed. I believe that understanding who we are and who we wish to be and the causes in our development that sets the standards for us personally as humans, is both important and necessary to a far better understanding of our selves and how we live our lives,

Thus enabling a progressive movement forward and away from emotional turmoil to assist in understanding of others and ourselves,

Thus developing stronger self Confidence .You must remember that in life there will always be somebody to envy and admire because they appear to do something better than you feel you could archive. This is being very judgmental of yourself. Without knowing their personal limits in life and feelings of what they can or cannot do and their own self judgment.

We as people can archive anything with understanding our own limits and how to apply our special individual talents, we are all very special and individuals. Feel good about yourself and seek help always if you are seemly pushed and unable to understand the out of control feeling and emotional changes in life. And one must remember that an understanding of unthought-of standards unconsciously sets a barrier of our personal standards

Always in life we should remember a pain shared is half the pain and a love shared is twice the love.